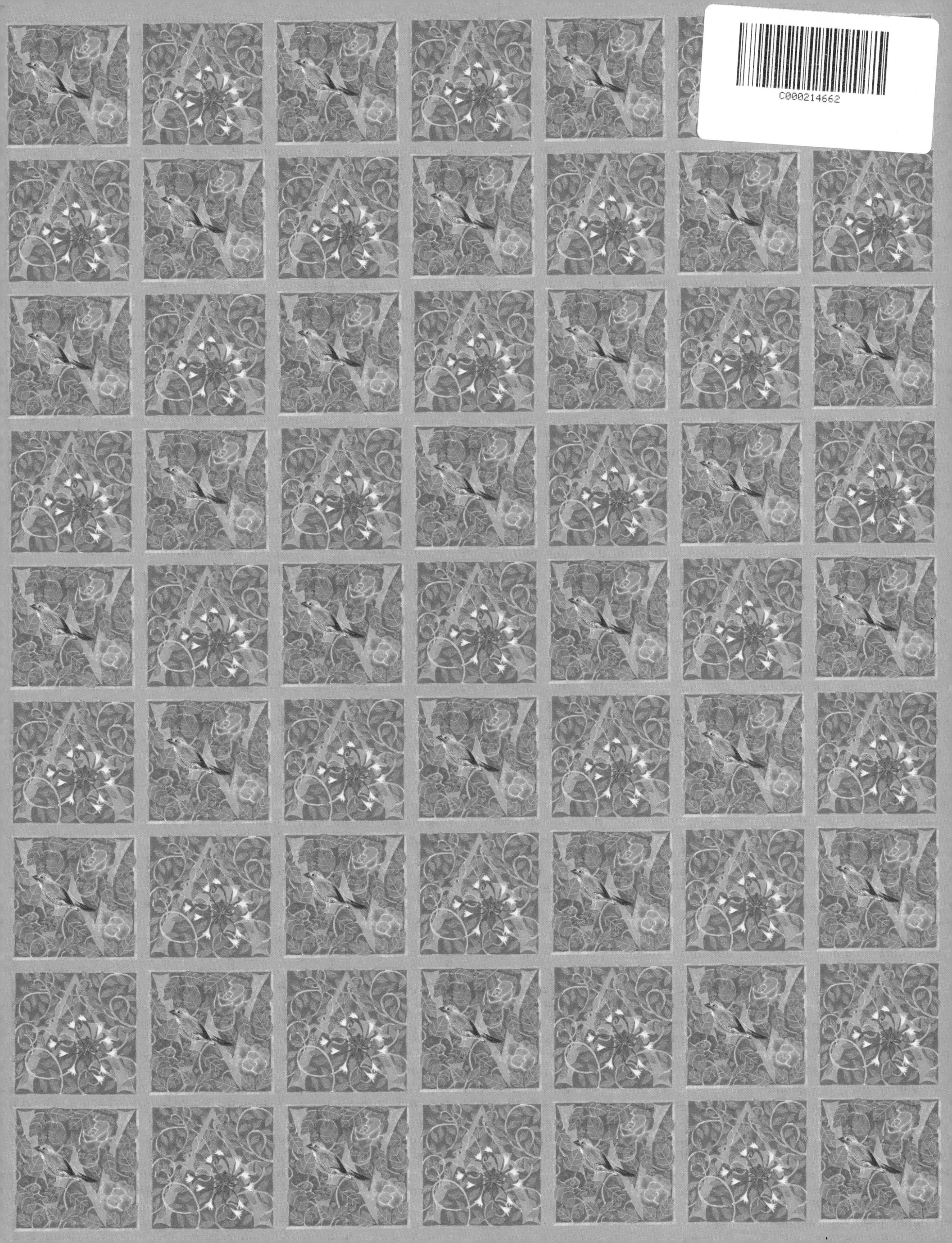

WIGMORE ABBEY

THE TREASURE OF MORTIMER

A PERSONAL ACCOUNT BY

JOHN CHALLIS

PHOTOGRAPHS BY

ALEX RAMSAY

WIGMORE BOOKS

CONTENTS

THE MORTIMERS

Reluctant as I am to subject readers to a long, possibly boring history lesson, I feel it would be helpful to give a brief historic outline of the region and the Mortimer family, who were responsible for founding and maintaining Wigmore Abbey, and who became one of the great English families of the Middle Ages.

The valley in which the abbey is set was probably hollowed by the fat icy finger of a glacier pushing its way south in the Devensian period of the last ice-age, 10,000 to 18,000 years ago. As this freezing invader retreated, it left a useful route for the early river Teme which, starting high in the Kerry Hills, served as a fast-flowing run off from there. At some point in its history, the river managed to work its way through the gorge at Downton, from where it continued towards Ludlow and around the mound on which the castle was built, before meandering down a broad valley to join the River Severn below Worcester.

The millennia of gentle flow of the river and its regular rising and flooding of the valley floor at Wigmore and further west around Brampton Bryan, have left it a fertile, alluvial tract of ground, which has probably been producing crops for its inhabitants since well before the Celts arrived around four thousand years ago.

No doubt over the centuries the sinuous course of the river has altered, but its banks still provide a much-valued venue for catchers of trout, grayling and salmon, who must wait years for old members to pass on before they can gain the right to cast a fly into the Leintwardine fisheries.

The Anglo-Saxon Chronicles tell us that in AD 921, the King Edward the Elder *'in the Rogation Days, commanded the Burgh at Wicingamere to be built'*, as a Saxon defence against the Celtic Britons who still occupied most of Wales. They also tell us that in the same year, this timber-walled fortress successfully resisted a siege by a great army of Danes.

Less than 150 years later, the first stone castle was built, one of the earlier examples using innovative Norman technology. Its new occupant and builder, William FitzOsbern, had arrived with King William I from Normandy. As part of the assertion of Norman control over Wales and the West, FitzOsbern was a major builder of Norman castles, including Carisbrooke on the Isle of Wight, Chepstow, Clifford in Herefordshire, Berkeley Castle in Gloucestershire and Monmouth Castle in Wales, as well as Wigmore. He also created or improved fortifications in the towns of Hereford and Shrewsbury, for which King William created him First Earl of Hereford.

The Conqueror, grateful for FitzOsbern's assistance in cowing the Saxons, granted to him substantial lands in the central Marches, on the edge of the so far unconquered Kingdom of Wales, in return for discouraging its natives from straying into England.

To achieve this effectively, he'd needed a strategic and easily defensible point of power. The site of Wigmore castle was a naturally defended rocky prominence, overlooking the broad valley of the Teme. Even today, if you clamber up the steep grassy ramp to the castle, half a mile beyond Wigmore's

11th century church of St James, enter through the still standing portcullis gate and, puffing harder all the time, trudge up through the tumbled masonry, destroyed in the seventeenth century by Cromwell's army, to the remnants of the keep, the advantage of its position is obvious, with clear views up and down the valley, and across it to the hills on the far side, and, as it happens, to our house, two miles away. Interestingly, the Normans were by no means the first soldiers to see the strategic benefits of the area. In the 2nd century AD the Romans had laid a road from north to south – a kind of early M5 which linked modern day Cheshire with South Wales. The nearest village to the abbey is Leintwardine, which was originally built by the Romans as Bravonium, a garrison town straddling their highway. The lay-out of the settlement and the ditches that defended it are still visible in parts.

Who first occupied the castle built by FitzOsbern is unclear, but it is recorded that at some point within twenty years of the Conquest, King William gave the Manor of Wigmore to another supporter. Compiled in 1086, the Domesday Book tells us that Wigmore Castle was held by one Ralph de Mortimer, who, it is said, had been granted the castle and its estates as a reward for putting down the Saxon resistance of Edric, Earl of Shrewsbury.

Ralph, reportedly a cousin of William I, was a member of a prominent Norman family. Some years after the conquest, Ralph crossed the channel to join William in dealing with the residual resistance of the conquered English. His contribution is not well recorded, but whatever he did was enough to merit the gift of an important castle in a key position.

For the next four centuries Wigmore Castle, along with vast borderland and Welsh estates which they'd acquired along the way, was to remain in Mortimer hands – the focal point for a very powerful family. In the early 1300s the much more impressive Ludlow Castle was added to their estates, when Roger, 3rd Baron Mortimer, married Joan de Genneville. Joan had inherited Ludlow and all its estates in her own right, and this was absorbed into the already substantial Mortimer holdings in England, Wales and Ireland. By 1320, Roger had moved his centre of operations to Ludlow.

Roger had been born in 1287 and at the age of 14 was married to Joan de Genneville as part of a deal done between their respective parents. For the next twenty years, theirs seems to have been an amenable marriage, Joan usually travelling with Roger while bearing him twelve children in the process.

Roger succeeded his father, Sir Edmund, Lord of Wigmore at the age of 16 in 1303. Three years later, he was summoned by King Edward I to Windsor, where along with about two hundred other young noblemen, he was knighted, in return for which he was expected to rally round and be chums with the young Prince Edward. He was made a ward of a young blood called Piers Gaveston who, already granted substantial holdings of land, had become very close to the prince. It is not known just how close Gaveston and Edward were, nor whether their love for one another was merely brotherly, or thoroughly

carnal. Whichever, Piers Gaveston was evidently a self-serving schemer (as well as the inspiration for the notorious 1970s Oxford club to which David Cameron, former Prime Minister, once belonged) and made the most of his relationship with the young prince, especially when Edward succeeded to the throne on his father's death in 1307.

The following year, Edward II travelled to France to marry Isabella, the twelve-year-old daughter of the King of France. He returned to find a reception party waiting for him, headed by Piers Gaveston. Roger Mortimer's wife, Joan was one of the ladies in the party of courtiers. Roger himself was a functionary at the English wedding that took place at Westminster.

The King and Queen made their way to Windsor, at a time when Edward wasn't sure what the rest of his barons thought of him. Roger was getting on well with Gaveston, his ward master, and took the opportunity to pledge his own support and generally suck up to the weak-willed king. This resulted in Roger being despatched to Ireland to keep order there in the king's name. He also acted in this capacity in Scotland, as well as establishing, with the help of his uncle Roger, Lord Mortimer of Chirk, a very tight grip on his own territories in Wales and the Marches.

Meanwhile, the glamorous Piers Gaveston, recently created 1st Earl of Cornwall by his doting royal chum, was making the most of the king's favour, and had begun really to get up the noses of a group of senior earls, and the King, bowing to heavy pressure from the noblemen, was obliged to send him to exile on three separate occasions.

Returning from his third period of exile in 1312, in the face of fierce opposition from the Church (he'd been excommunicated), a gang of nobles headed by the Earl of Lancaster, hunted him, caught him and took him to Oxford where they had him summarily executed by two Welshmen.

After the death of Gaveston, who had been an ally of Roger's, Roger further ingratiated himself with the king, and remained as a key presence around the court, when he wasn't away looking after the king's interests.

At court, the ambitious and unscrupulous Hugh Despenser had also recognised the vacancy in the King's neediness, and started to wheedle himself into the favour of the unpopular monarch. At the same time, Despenser was making enemies in Wales by trying to muscle in on the holdings of the established Marcher Lords, including some of Roger Mortimer's territory in Carmarthen.

A lot of the English barons were becoming annoyed with Despenser's growing influence as Lord Chamberlain, now controlling access to the king. While Roger had got along with Gaveston, his growing personal animosity towards Despenser, as a result of his land-grabbing activities, had now engendered within him a growing sense of grievance towards the king.

He became part of an all-out rebellion, alongside several other major nobles, but this came to a head for him after a battle in Shrewsbury in 1322. Facing defeat by Edward's forces, he was tricked into surrendering with his older uncle, Lord Mortimer of Chirk.

They both had all their possessions confiscated and were banged up in the Tower of London. However, they managed a dramatic – not to say spectacular – escape by drugging their jailers, and Roger fled to France in August 1323, pursued by warrants for his capture, dead or alive.

Although Queen Isabella over nine years, from the age of 17 to 26 had managed to bear King Edward four children, including two sons, she had by then become less enamoured of him and his fondness, first, for Gaveston, and then Despenser. A couple of years after Roger had got himself out of the tower, she booked herself out of Edward's court, on the pretext of travelling to the country of her birth on a specious diplomatic mission. She had almost certainly seen quite a bit of Roger Mortimer over the years since she'd first arrived at the English court; Roger's wife, Joan, had been one of her ladies in waiting. Isabella would have recognised in Roger a far more potent man than her husband, and it seems likely that a latent affair between them had been smouldering for some time. When they met up again in France, Joan had remained in England with the children and Roger hadn't seen her for almost four years, so the relationship blossomed with a passion, leading Isabella and Roger to a hatch a plot to return to England to confront the King, depose him, and put his eldest son, Prince Edward, on the throne.

When Isabella and Mortimer landed at the mouth of the River Orwell in Suffolk in September 1326, they were greeted enthusiastically, aided by Henry, Earl of Lancaster, and given a lot of support. King Edward soon caved in and fled to Wales but was caught and incarcerated at Berkeley Castle by the Severn in Gloucestershire. It was here that he was alleged to have received the infamous red-hot poker treatment from which it was believed that he had died – not surprisingly. His body was never officially identified though, and there were alternative reports of him – like Shergar and Lord Lucan – being seen wandering about Europe. Some believe he was imprisoned in Corfe Castle in Dorset.

Edward and Isabella's eldest son was crowned Edward III in January 1327, at the age of 13. As they had planned, Isabella and Mortimer were appointed as the juvenile king's regents, with all the power they could have wished for, and in 1328, the young king agreed to Roger being created Earl of March.

He returned regularly to his home territory in the Marches, and the evidence of that is still very visible

today. In a mood of vanity, he had built within the inner bailey of Ludlow Castle a magnificent Great Chamber block – a suite of entertaining rooms, a state of the art lavatory block and apartments, in which he was able to entertain his lover, the Queen Isabella, and her son, the king.

However, his growing power began to be resented by angry and jealous nobles, including his former ally, the Earl of Lancaster. They tried to overthrow Mortimer, but with no result as the young king refused to get involved. Subsequently, however, in March 1330, when Mortimer ordered the execution of Edmund, Earl of Kent, Edward II's half-brother, Lancaster talked the young king into asserting himself. In October 1330, a Parliament was summoned to Nottingham, a few days before Edward's eighteenth birthday. When Mortimer and Isabella turned up they were seized and held by Edward and his supporters.

Although Isabella begged her son to be gentle with Roger Mortimer, Mortimer was banged up in the Tower – again. Accused of assuming royal powers and other acts of treason, he was condemned without trial and ignominiously hanged at Tyburn on 29 November 1330, his vast estates forfeited to the crown. His body hung at the gallows for two days and nights in full view of the people, to discourage any more threats to the young king's rule. Isabella had Roger's body buried at Greyfriars in Coventry after the hanging.

Mortimer's widow, Joan de Genneville, who had been punished for no more than simply being Roger's wife, received a pardon in 1336 and survived till 1356.

Six and a half centuries later, in 2002, the BBC TV's *House Detectives at Large* came to investigate the abbot's lodging at Wigmore, now our home. During the investigation, a document was discovered showing that Joan had petitioned Edward III for the return of her husband's body so she could bury it at Wigmore Abbey.

Edward III had replied, 'Let his body rest in peace.' Later, the king relented, and Mortimer's body was reported to have been moved to Wigmore Abbey, where Joan was later buried beside him. However, their grave has never been identified, nor has Roger's presence at Wigmore been confirmed. A very limited amount of digging was allowed for the TV programme, and no sign of the burial was found. It is possible that Roger's remains were, in fact, never brought here, and one day they will re-appear from beneath a car-park in Coventry.

THE ABBEY

THE HISTORY OF the Abbey of St James at Wigmore begins some sixty years after the Normans annexed our island, when Sir Oliver de Merlimond, mentor and agent to Ralph de Mortimer, decided to rebuild an existing wooden chapel in stone on lands granted to him by Ralph at Shobdon, some five or six miles to the South-west of Wigmore. Once the project was under way, he was prompted to undertake a pilgrimage to the shrine of St James at Santiago de Compostela, in northern Spain. On his way home through northern France, he met a canon from the Monastery of St Victor in Normandy.

Asked back to the monastery, well-known at the time for its religious and intellectual achievements, Sir Oliver was deeply impressed by what he saw. Back home in Shobdon, he determined to found a monastery based on his newly built church, and invited the Abbot of St Victor to send monks to establish a 'satellite' priory there. This was to be the first 'Victorine' house in England – a monastery established under the Augustinian Rule in the manner of its Norman mother house.

Regrettably, though, Oliver fell out badly with his new overlord, Ralph's son, Hugh de Mortimer, who grabbed back the Shobdon estate and summarily turfed the two Victorine canons out of their new priory.

However, the Bishop of Hereford persuaded Hugh to found a monastery, which he promised, but initially failed to do, and the Canons went back to France.

After some no doubt persistent badgering from the Abbot of St Victor, Hugh capitulated and agreed to keep to his word and take them back, finding a site for the new monastery at Eye, a few miles south of the castle on the River Lugg. The new establishment was still being built when in the uncertain conditions of a simmering civil war, Mortimer was concerned that it might be fortified and become a threat, so the canons were shuffled up the old Roman road to Wigmore, housed there and told to use St James's Church. They were not happy – either with the accommodation they'd been allocated, or with the trudge up the hill several times a day to perform their monastic duties.

The monks evidently decided to sort out a more satisfactory solution and eventually identified a site for a proper monastery on the far side of the valley. They secured it from Hugh de Mortimer's son, also Hugh, who had succeeded to the Wigmore estates in 1153. This Hugh put up timber buildings for the brethren, but decided in 1171 to make a more permanent structure in stone. Paying for the construction himself, he laid the foundation stone, and it was completed by 1179.

Hugh ended up becoming a monk himself (possibly abbot) and was buried in front of the High Altar. Under the arch of the gatehouse, we found a lead plaque, placed there in the 19th century, listing those Mortimers thought to have been buried somewhere in our garden. After the arch of the south transept had been restored by us (with help from English Heritage) we moved the plaque and had it set in a piece of stone at the base of the transept.

The abbey church was cruciform in shape, with transepts and a vaulted nave about 100 feet long. Today, very little of the church remains, the south transept arch being the largest standing piece – the stone finger of masonry pointing at the sky that Carol and I had spotted across the misty meadow from our car while parked in the rutted remains of the Roman road.

While not much of the church is left, the remnants of decorative stone carving – chevron, dog-tooth and foliage – indicate the opulence of its construction, and the French influence of the mother house of St Victor.

By the fifteenth century, after three hundred years of existence, the abbey was looking shabby. An outside report in 1424 indicates that it had reached a low point in its fortunes. The buildings and barns were in a sorry state, and the abbey itself run down, with dogs fouling everywhere and the local population using the cloisters as a urinal. It was in little better shape a hundred years later, as Henry VIII was preparing his stand off against Pope Clement VII in order to satisfy his urge to marry the coquettish and self-promoting Ann Boleyn.

The last Abbot of Wigmore, John Smart, had been elected in November 1518 and installed by the bishop of Hereford. In 1530, one of his canons, John Lee sent Thomas Cromwell a damning indictment of the abbot, who he claimed had been ordaining unsuitable men as priests, on a huge scale, a thousand at a time, earning, it was claimed, a pound a head. Despite this obvious abuse of his position, on the suppression of his monastery, the abbot was granted a hefty pension of £80 per year.

The abbey buildings were granted to a series of individuals until, in 1556, Queen Mary granted the remaining buildings and land in perpetuity to Philip Cockeram, with whose heirs it remained until 1744, when a Cockeram bequeathed it to his relations, the Salweys of Richard's Castle.

GHOSTS & LEGENDS

Documented with less academic rigour than the story of the buildings themselves, is the history of the ghosts of Wigmore Abbey. There is, of course, no shortage of rumour. Naturally, a Grey Lady has been seen, as well as a more unusual spectre, a pipe-smoking old gent, the smell of whose pungent tobacco smoke is said to have awoken sleeping parents, and led them into the adjoining bedroom, where their small child was about to be asphyxiated by his little pillow – a decent, public-spirited sort of ghost, unlike the Grey Lady, whose manifestation was more malevolent and generally tiresome – slamming doors, knocking things off their perches, though occasionally trying to make amends by producing an overpowering scent of pot-pourri at the top of the stairs.

And there was the 'Watcher' – discernible from particular spots in the garden, towards dusk at the witching hour – a presence at the old mullioned window set high on the southern wall of the abbot's parlour, sometimes accompanied by a sudden sharp gust of wind, vigorously shaking the lilac, while all around everything was still.

Along with the ghosts are the legends, for a place like this could not have stood for eight hundred years without generating its own mythology. A much-vaunted story, followed up from time to time by intrepid archaeologists is that of the 'tunnel' – a passageway said to have run the mile or so across the valley from Wigmore Castle, ancient stronghold of the Mortimers, to the abbey drain below the undercroft.

The drain certainly existed, indeed, is still visible in part, built to channel away the steady inflow of groundwater, as well as the effluent from the abbot's garderobe, before being flushed out into the marshy valley floor. A man could walk upright along it, beneath the farmyard for about a hundred feet, until brought to a halt by a major fall completely blocking the way, after which it was presumed to turn left towards the higher ground and the castle. Evidence of a tunnel has been found closer to the castle, when farmers' ploughs have revealed facing stones on their ends, as if supporting the roof, a passage, a kind of 'cut & cover', probably topped with hurdles and earth in the earlier days, and providing a hidden exit from the castle in case of invasion.

Another tantalising rumour has it that a right fork in the drain led to a second tunnel that ended up at the nunnery, a few hundred yards towards the river.

The drain/passage under the western end of the abbot's lodging is one of the oldest parts of the building, and there was great excitement over the identification of the double Norman arch at the

Image courtesy English Heritage

entrance to the drainage channels. It was the partial collapse of this drain that caused some instability in the south west corner of the building, leading to the need for iron ties and straps to hold it together, as well as the insertion of Victorian brick pillars to shore up the ancient walls. During one of several archaeological visits that have been made, I did take the opportunity to walk upright along the tunnel for about fifty feet, looking up the various shafts that pierced the roof, through which unmentionable fluids were poured in the days before health and safety directives had come to brighten our lives.

Sad to say, in the seventeen years since Carol and I have lived in the abbey, no ghouls or spectres, grey ladies or ethereal pipe-smokers have taken the trouble to manifest themselves. Could it be that we are just too worldly for these phantoms to consider us receptive? Nevertheless, the factual history of the building is less fanciful, and has fascinated us since we arrived, always eager and ready to learn more. After exchanging contracts for the purchase of our pile of venerable stone, we'd been given a box full of musty old pieces of parchment and vellum, strewn with dangling wax seals and indecipherable, drunk spider writing, all of which was invaluable in piecing together more of the history of the place. The basic facts, revealed by these historical documents and the residual archaeology, are straightforward enough and have given us a colourful if incomplete picture of the abbey's history.

REFURBISHMENT

THE REMAINS OF the abbot's lodgings make an extraordinary house, started in the twelfth century but added to, changed, botched, reinforced over the centuries that followed. Although the lodgings had survived as a dwelling after Henry VIII had ordered the destruction of the greater part of the monasteries in the land, the passing of time has revealed sporadic signs of instability and the structure had been suitably propped up by stone buttresses, and, in Victorian times, strapped and tied with forged iron braces.

To describe the structure of the place, I will, with his kind permission, quote from a six-page article on Wigmore Abbey written by John Goodall, architectural editor of *Country Life*. This was a comprehensively researched piece which examined the origins of the monastery, as well as the curious succession of owners following the Dissolution. It appeared in the issue of January 29th 2014.

> *The surviving medieval remains comprise two ranges, set end to end to the south west of the church. One is of timber frame and incorporates a magnificent gateway of stone. The other grange is enclosed by thick stone walls and preserves a zany array of medieval windows, many of them clearly moved to their present position since the dissolution.*
>
> *A hall with a fine open roof occupies one end of the stone range. Tree-ring dating of its timbers suggest that it was erected in the 1480s. The remainder of the range has been divided horizontally to create undercrofts and two upper floors. Many of the timbers incorporated in the fabric are clearly recycled from other buildings. Tree-ring dating suggests a complex evolution of the present internal arrangements and panelling with important changes in about 1680 and 1730. It was probably in conjunction with the first round of changes that a cross range with fine chimneys was added to the east end of the stone monastic range. And, during the second, that parts of the building were refenestrated with sash windows.*

While my first impression of the gentle, melancholy old building was that it looked like a badly-wrapped parcel, its stones and timbers gave it a sense of permanence and tranquillity that seemed to exhale its eight hundred years of history. It was being lived in when we first found it, and over the previous twenty years it had been 'modernised'- at least, a rudimentary effort had been made to botch up any damage that had become apparent. Where the plaster hadn't been replaced with hardboard panels, it was painted stark white. Some of the ancient oak balustrading had been replaced with varnished brown pine. In other parts the grey stone walls stood undressed, in rocky nakedness. They cried out for warm colours, care and gentle understanding.

When we arrived at Wigmore Abbey on 23 July 1998, we both knew we'd entered a critical new phase of our lives. We welcomed it and were committed to it, although I found it quite disorienting. Unlike Carol, I'd never lived in proper country and wasn't prepared even for some of the more minor changes from urban life. For instance, it took me a long time to get used to the general absence of street lighting, even in some of the villages.

And while I was used to a certain amount of birdsong in the leafy purlieus of East Sheen, the racket a feathered chorus can kick up of a summer's dawn among the spinneys and hedges of this deeply rustic corner of England came as a shock. I had to get used to the lack of traffic in the lane that passed our house. The few vehicles that we saw were largely of an agricultural nature and I learned the hard way, with a few near misses, that single-track lanes with ditches, thick hedges or solid banks don't allow for errors of judgement, especially involving tractors with six furrow ploughs on the back.

From the moment we arrived there, I loved where I lived – the horizons of rolling, wooded hills, the daytime peace broken by the keening of buzzards wheeling in an empty sky, the air heavy with the aroma of grass, cattle, sheep dung and fox. But it took me a long time to feel that I wasn't an impostor or an incomer with no right to be there. I felt I was polluting this beautiful, peaceful innocent country with my nasty urban, showbiz ways. In fact, it was a good two or three years before I felt I had really bedded in and become a genuine part of my surroundings.

In the meantime, one of our first tasks was to invite English Heritage, official custodians of ancient monuments, to make a long overdue visit to the abbey when we could introduce ourselves and find out more about the responsibilities we were taking on.

The ruins of the abbey church itself – a south nave and transept – were in a parlous state, and we guessed that the conservation of these was the most pressing job. The Abbey is a Scheduled Ancient Monument, with the abbot's lodging – our new home – listed as Grade I – further proof, if that were needed, that this was a very special place. Deeply picturesque, built of stone hewn from the nearby hills and mellowed by winds gusting up the ancient glacial valley for the last eight hundred years, it exudes a sense of permanence and peace. The inner, half-timbered fourteenth century gatehouse is unique (and has been much sketched over the years, perhaps most strikingly by John Piper).

There was a great deal to do but our first priority was the reordering of the abbot's lodgings, which we wanted to make into a comfortable home, but as a Grade I listed building, there were obviously constraints on what we could do to it and the materials we should use. We didn't mind; we understood that it had to be done appropriately, but we were soon to find out just how pernickety English Heritage could be.

It turned out that they had been itching to get their boots on to the site for years, while successive owners had denied them access. Now we let them in: they came, they saw, they fussed, they monitored.

Our own first major decision over the building work was motivated as much by philanthropy as anything else. An old friend of Carol's had recently married a man who was experiencing a hiatus in his business activity, along with an associated cash-flow crisis; he was urgently looking for a new project. He was one of those small-scale 'property developers' who were then operating around the outer fringes of smart London, rooting out small cheap houses in Victorian terraces which, with some minor cosmetic attention, would scrub up well enough to sell on at a bit of a profit.

With hindsight – very vivid hindsight, as it turned out – this was not a good basis for employing a man

JOHN PIPER,
The Gatehouse of Wigmore Abbey.
By kind permission of the John Piper Trust

in Tenbury Wells. The Herbery gave us great encouragement and became a large part of our plan, along with the wild flowers they also cultivate. When we first found them, they were living in a cottage which stood in deep country, by a tumbling brook, surrounded by a rambling herb and wildflower garden, either side of the lane that runs down to a little ford over the stream, before rising again through woodland towards Tenbury.

Dedicated people with a wry humour and a fount of knowledge, Rob and Kim are joint authors of a fascinating book, *Hidden Histories of Herbs*, revealing little known properties of over one hundred and fifty plants.

Thus we'd identified the source of plants for our own herb garden; later it also provided all the plants for Lavender Hill, which we conceived around the base of the ruined south transept wall of the Abbey.

Another source of inspiration was a chance meeting with Charles Chesshire on one of our garden walks. Charles is a renowned expert on garden design with an encyclopaedic knowledge of trees and, more particularly for us, clematis. On a series of garden walks in places like How Caple in Herefordshire and Painswick in Gloucestershire we explored arboreta and boned up on clematis.

At that time, Charles was running the garden centre at Burford House near Tenbury Wells, and this

JC and Rob Hurst from Cottage Herbery

Dave Bufton

became the source of much of our clematis. His knowledge and advice were invaluable, contrasting the advantages of 'drifts' of one colour, with the 'one of each' approach.

Several varieties of Clematis were essential to our vision of how the gardens around Wigmore Abbey should look. Their ability to scramble and light up already spent shrubs, and fill ugly spaces was crucial to our plan. Charles with his quizzical look and somewhat dark humour provided just the right sort of encouragement.

In fact, we took advice from wherever it was offered – magazines, newspaper articles, opinions from experts casually encountered – Monty Don (met, bizarrely, at a medieval picnic in Usk Castle in Monmouthshire), Alan Titchmarsh at the Chelsea Flower show and Sir Roy Strong at his garden, The Laskett, at Much Birch in South Herefordshire.

Often our garden visits in the area would point us in the right direction to find the plants we needed: David Austin for roses, his daughter Claire for irises and Kelways for peonies (a particular favourite) while Matthews in Tenbury Wells were highly recommended for fruit trees.

Two large, special nurseries provided many of the plants we were keen to experiment with – from hellebore to helenium, philadelphus to pittosporum. We loved the pittosporum for its pale green-veined delicacy, although, sadly for us, it proved too delicate for our weather-prone position in the bottom of the Teme valley. Twice we tried it; twice it succumbed to the vicissitudes of the English winter.

On our hunt for rarities, we'd been advised to head up to Crug Plants in deepest North Wales. We arrived

after us. They were, I believe, one of the first garden centres to make up whole large pots for their customers, as well as complete hanging baskets.

With such a large area of garden to cover, we were keen to find practical, versatile shrubs that would, ideally, give us the three big reasons to be cheerful: foliage; flower; fruit or berries.

We also needed hedging, and ground cover, but we needed it to be worth looking at, too. Osmanthus, for example, was evergreen, flowered early, was highly scented and hedged well. Viburnum and philadelphus were always favourites, so it was a bonus to find that both flourished in our stony soil, and the way that all our roses took to us was thrilling

We were delighted that we'd been able to find so much of what we wanted at our two favourite nurseries, Crug and Derwen.

to oooh and aaah at a host of beautifully unusual things, like woodruff, thalictrum and tiarella. Some worked, some didn't; with these kinds of plants, it seems, you never know until you've tried them. One plant might not work because we'd planted it where the conifers once stood and the ground was too acidic and covered in pine needles; another might work for a short time – perhaps a couple of years – before giving up and disappearing, but others, thank goodness, have survived and thrived.

At the excellent Dingle Nurseries near Welshpool, two whole hillsides are taken up by all manner of trees and shrubs, perennials and annuals. Here we found we could easily spend most of a day, sometimes in the company of the founder, a twinkly-eyed rapscallion of advanced years with a great stock of tales to tell. Sadly, no longer with us, he was a vivid reminder of how the business of plant growing and nurture was run before the emergence of the highly commercial, pile 'em high set-ups that dominate the retail plant market today.

On the way back from the Dingle was the Derwen Garden Centre, another family-run business, where 'Nothing's too much Trouble' Neville always looks

In the years that we've spent conceiving, planting and nurturing our garden, it has evolved as a series of distinct spaces, or 'rooms', inspired in part by our visits to Sissinghurst.

One area that has required regular adjustment over that time has been the Cloister Garden, so named because of its position to the south of the nave wall, and west of the remains of the south transept. We found here a serenity that differed from the other more exposed parts of the garden, reflecting the sense of ordered calm that may have pervaded the place eight centuries before. We imagined contemplative monks strolling around its perimeter, which suggested a more formal approach to the lay-out.

When we first inspected it to make some kind of plan, the meadow grass was growing right up to the nave wall. The crumbling wall, still about eighteen feet high, looked as if it were being held up by a combination of the ivy, elder and ash saplings that sprawled all over it.

Hacking our way through to the bottom of the ancient stone structure, we suddenly noticed a blood red rose protruding from the greenery, right at the top of the wall. Further investigation revealed an ancient Park Direktor Riggers, almost skeletal at the base, but after thrusting its way up through the robust foliage towards the light, it had defiantly produced this one jewel of a flower.

'Here I am!' it seemed to be saying. What a thrill it was to provide some light and a little air to a great survivor – at least thirty to forty years old, by the look of the gnarled old stem at the bottom.

We reflected that red roses had been powerful symbols for many monasteries, as representing the blood of Christ, and this gave us a lead on how to present this section of the garden.

To reproduce a sense of the medieval cloisters, we would plant borders on two sides, leave the eastern end open to take advantage of the dramatic remains of the south transept, and close the southern edge with a yew hedge. Yew has been considered sacred for thousands of years and has strong connections with many ecclesiastical buildings. For the square which the edges contained, we decided on four grass panels, each with a Versailles-type planter in its centre, with gravel paths leading from the edges and meeting in the middle at a central feature. And we had to decide what this might be. A fountain seemed too over the top; we already had a statue in the raised garden. Eventually we found a great stone bowl, perhaps an

ancient, abandoned font, sitting in the long grass at a remote reclamation centre. Our friend, Dee Hardwicke who is an artist and micro-mosaic expert with a studio in Monmouth was inspired by the design and colour of an old floor tile from the abbey and made a roundel to cover the base of the font, which also acts as a birdbath and is a source of frequent admiration.

Directly fronting the eastern elevation of what was now the house we occupied there was an area which had been enclosed by the dorter (the monks' sleeping quarters) and the frater (the refectory) – perhaps another, secondary cloister – but more likely to have been a multi-use courtyard. This space had been filled with rubble from the ruined monastery, mainly in the 17th century, when games lawns were all the rage – for playing bowls, or croquet, perhaps. The place had been filled in to a depth of about eight feet, forming a raised platform on which the meadow had spread itself and now flourished. For this space, too, we

Photo © Jesse Wild

Dee Hardwicke, ceramic artist

wanted some formality, and aimed to achieve this by mowing two cruciform paths, leaving four panels of meadow. We left the eastern edge wild, allowing it to 'bleed' into the lower meadow beyond a ha-ha which some former pretentious owner had created. We knew this was a potential risky plan in that it would require a certain degree of high maintenance, though, we thought this a small price to pay for the thrill of seeing the meadow flowers in spring, inching their way up through the grasses – clover, speedwell, vetches, to which we added narcissi, tulips and alliums. Now it comes every year, as pleasing as ever to anticipate and witness.

To the south of this area was what we had come to call the Summer House garden, as its most prominent feature was the old stone folly we had recovered from a sea of shrubbery. Here we found we had inherited the bones of a more formal garden, consisting of two rectangular beds, surrounded by dilapidated paved pathways. Having found this (possibly Victorian) piece of the abbey's history, our first instinct was to change everything, dig up the decrepit paving, rotovate the soil, reduce everything to ground zero and start again – but how?

Vegetables! we thought – though not for long.

I'd already tried that on an allotment back in North Sheen, where I used to live in South West London. At the time, my career was undergoing something of a hiatus – or, to put it bluntly, nobody seemed to need my services as an actor – so I thought I'd take the opportunity to do something I'd always wanted to do, and grow some of my own food. I soon learned that this is a rich man's hobby, when, following the rule of Sod's Law, as soon as I'd got going, the phone started ringing with offers of work, and I was far too busy for vegetable growing. In any case, during the short time I was at it, I found I produced copious quantities of lettuce, radishes, spring onions and Brussels sprouts that all came to fruition at the exact moment they were at rock bottom prices in the shops, which made a bit of a mockery of all the effort I'd put into it. At the same time, I reminded myself, nothing beats the taste of home-grown veg, fresh from your own soil, the fruit of your labour. As a natural pessimist, it's never easy launching into a new project, but at least it avoids disappointment; if it doesn't work, you knew it wouldn't work; if it does work, you are pleasantly surprised. Perhaps this streak in me explains why Eeyore was my favourite in *Winnie the Pooh*, rather than the insufferable Tigger or the foolish Piglet.

Now, considering the options for the Summer House garden, the idea of being enslaved by a vegetable garden, or potager, was unthinkable. It was widely known what a tyranny they could become, albeit interspersed with sporadic joys, earned through true dedication and very hard work. We found much more appeal in creating the haphazard informality of the continuous tapestry of roses, clematis and peonies, following snowdrops, narcissus and osmanthus, leading on to crocosmia, helenium, and Michelmas daisy, via tradescantia and Japanese anemone. With so much to plant and to discover, we just knew we'd have no time for vegetables. Besides, we loved the little summer house, from whose doorway was one of the great views of the garden back towards the

abbot's lodging. In keeping with that view, vegetables seemed far too prosaic. We decided to leave untouched the summer house and its special atmosphere in this corner of the garden, where you could imagine the people who had enjoyed this private place for over two hundred years. It was a place to read, or write poetry, or practise your speeches, or commune with ancient spirits. And thus it was decided, the only appropriate surrounding for this place was the changing patchwork, set between the ancient walkways.

A walk through what became the Summer House Garden, revealed an old timber door in a stone wall, which gave on to a cobbled enclosure, used, perhaps in Victorian times, as a cattle byre. Beyond it lay an area of unofficial grazing for our neighbouring farmer's stock, which had once been an orchard, but had become a rippling, impenetrable sea of thistles, nettles and brambles which had crept up to the wall to obscure the cobbles beneath. We were soon determined to reinstate the orchard it had once been.

I'd always wanted an orchard. As a boy, I had spent some happy times in my great-uncle Lewis Clapp's Somerset cider orchards in North Cadbury, near Shepton Mallet. Lewis was a mischievous farmer, race-horse breeder and practical joker. He had a sharp sense of humour which he demonstrated in calling his most famous horse The Wicked Uncle. The cider he produced was dangerously potent – something which I discovered when I was given my first tankard full at the age of nine. Quickly conking out, I was covered in hay and reported missing by Lewis. When my distraught mother asked him where I might be, he replied, 'I ain't seen 'im. I thought he was with you.'

Since those days, I'd always retained a warm relationship with orchards, apples and cider.

Shortly before Christmas, not long after the pilot episode was cut and ready, the BBC announced that they wanted us. The series was to be called *The Green, Green Grass*. We were scheduled to start making the other five episodes of the first series of the show during May and June 2005. But we also had to address the ticklish business of the location fee for the house. The producer had sent down a recce team to prepare the way. Our house became *Winterdown Farm* and photos were taken of the rooms inside so that something similar could be produced for the interior studio recording in Teddington.

On 1 September, almost exactly 24 years after *Boycie*'s first appearance on *Only Fools*, the first episode of *The Green, Green Grass* was aired and achieved over nine and a half million viewers – an amazing result at the time.

This sort of figure, however, wasn't expected to last. And it didn't. As viewers who had been hoping that David Jason and Nick Lyndhurst were going to be part of the action found that they weren't, we lost about a million and a half for the second episode, with numbers eventually settling at six and a half to seven million. Under the new conditions of widespread multi-channel viewing, this was considered better than expected, and things looked very positive.

We had enjoyed using the house and filming locally, and the four series of the show that were shot there had contributed healthily to the apparent never-ending costs of bringing the fabric of the house up to scratch.

Naturally, it was fun seeing the old place appearing on the screen, but our garden was given a better airing when the BBC chose to do a small feature on it during their coverage of the Chelsea Flower Show in 2010. Alan Titchmarsh, riding high with his afternoon show, was the BBC's leading anchor for Chelsea, and one spring day a crew pitched up to film the fruits of our labour in the garden. This was especially pleasing to us, because almost everything they showed were products of our own initiative and seemed to be meeting with broad approval.

While the making of the garden was more or less all our own work – or where not our own sweated labour, at least our own concept – the house had evolved over eight hundred years, and we were anxious to retain the integrity of the abbot's lodging. In any case the building's listed status imposed a number of constraints. One can't, with a listed house, just do what one wants for the sake of convenience, like shifting walls and windows around in a way that might jeopardise the historical fabric of the place; this didn't trouble us too much and we'd been happy to make compromises on our convenience and for the sake of the house's authenticity.

Owning, caring for, loving and living in an old, historically important building can give rise to a number of conflicting emotions. On the one hand one is very happy to be living in a place steeped in history, surrounded by a garden that seems to offer unlimited scope, and infinite joy; on the other is the absolutely relentless responsibility and (it must be said) expense involved in maintaining the structure of the house and the gardens, where none of the plants are polite enough to hang around, putting their growth in abeyance until one has a convenient moment to deal with it.

Another conflict exists between the desire to share this small, evidential piece of history with anyone else who is interested, and the hassle of having hordes of people trailing around the house, frequently asking questions one has been asked a hundred times before. We have no obligation to open the house, although we will by appointment, and generally we do try to allow access to small groups when it doesn't conflict too directly with our own activities. Carol, who is one of life's natural pâtissières, has in the past baked cakes for visiting parties, which we discovered only encouraged them back, for more treats.

On a less stressful level, we do still entertain the odd group to a short tour of the house (with jokes) and the garden (with Latin names). But for the most part we are now enjoying the house and the gardens which seem to have come through those tricky teenage years, and are settling down into reasonably decorous adulthood, although, of course, as with most gardens, if you give them their head and don't handle them with a certain degree of discipline, they can quickly go feral and drive you mad.

We have at least, over the past eighteen years, gently coaxed the house and its surroundings into a more or less stable condition. We have enjoyed almost every minute of it, and our affection for the charming, shambolic collection of old stones and windows has not diminished one jot – far from it – and despite the ongoing commitment it demands, we look forward to enjoying a peaceful, crepuscular interlude in our lives – until the next call comes!

THE GARDEN AT WIGMORE ABBEY
1 Gatehouse
2 Herb Garden
3 Nave Garden
4 Lavender Hill
5 Summerhouse Garden
6 Orchard
7 Joan's Garden
Woodland walk
I
7
6
N
S

2
3
4
5
2015